DESIGN AND MAKE
LOOSE
COVERS

HEATHER LUKE

For Sarah, Jackie, Julie, Chris, Liz, Lucy, Helen, Judi, Lisa and Charlotte

Published by Silverdale books
an imprint of Bookmart Ltd in 2001

Bookmart Ltd.
Desford Road
Enderby
Leicester LE9 5AD

Registered Number 2372865

ISBN 1 85605 647 3

Managing Editor: Coral Walker
Photographer: John Freeman
Designed by: Grahame Dudley Associates
Illustrations: Clare Davies

Reproduction by CMYK Ltd. South Africa
Printed and bound in Malaysia by
Times Offest (m) Sdn. Bhd.

10 9 8 7 6 5 4 3 2 1

ACKNOWLEDGEMENTS
With thanks to the following fabric companies for their help:
Page 5 LeLivre; page 20 Bennison; page 24 Osborne and Little;
page 30 Bennison; page 35 Pierre Frey - rug, De La Cuona - shawl;
page 36 Pierre Frey - cushion, De La Cuona - shawl; page 37 Bennison;
page 41 Pierre Frey - bottom left; page 46 Bennison;
page 50 Percheron - toile de jouy; page 59 Titley and Marr;
page 60 Le Lievre - top right; page 71 Bennison and Pierre Frey.

My personal thanks to John Freeman for his dedicated photographs,
to Gillian, Coral and all those at New Holland who have carefully steered
this book from conception to birth. To the brilliant seamstresses from my team
past and present - Chris Amey, Julie Toop, Sarah Westcott, and Jackie Pullman
who made the slipcovers. And heartfelt appreciation from us all, to Dibby
Nethercott, Mary Stewart-Wilson, Elizabeth Peck, Carol Hicks, and Heather
Phelps Brown for allowing us to photograph their lovely homes and without whose
support this book would certainly not have been possible.

CONTENTS

INTRODUCTION 4

BASIC TECHNIQUES 6

PREPARATION 10

MEASURING AND PLANNING 12

TAILORED COVERS 14

VALANCES 20

ARM SHAPES 25

QUILTING 32

CUSHIONS 34

FINISHING DETAILS 38

WOOD FRAMES 42

DAY BEDS 50

KITCHEN AND DINING CHAIRS 52

GARDEN CHAIRS 64

STOOLS 70

DRAPED COVERS 74

GLOSSARY 79

INDEX 80

INTRODUCTION

Deliciously overdone, this fantastic weft-woven silk transforms an old bentwood chair into a dressing table chair to be envied.

Casual, easy-clean and adaptable – loose covers are now much more acceptable in the home as the fashion in furnishings reflects the increased informality of clothing and other areas of lifestyle. Confusingly, a loose cover may be fitted, loose or it can be draped. Although rather a contradiction in terms, you can make a cover to fit so tightly it will be indistinguishable from an upholstered cover. Alternatively, it can be loose enough to slip on and off, or even draped and styled to follow its own interpretation.

Your period of home and preferred style of furnishing will have the most influence, but fashion and furnishing trends should be considered so that your ideas are not quickly outdated. Watch particularly for trends in mixing colours and fabrics. Choose a tone just deeper than the main fabric for a formal cover, a soft tone with a floral pattern or self-piping for an informal cover, and a check or stripe on the cross for impact.

Just as warm, dark colours complement the atmosphere of short grey days, so light airy furnishings reflect the long, light days. Here, loose covers come into their own as several sets made in various colours and fabrics can be slipped on and off easily with each changing season.

Loose cover-making skills are not difficult to master. Each day I am lucky enough to see the transformation of old-fashioned and ugly pieces of furniture into things of real beauty as a single flat length of fabric is cut, snipped, fitted and stitched in the hands of an expert. And I am always amazed when teaching new students how quickly and accurately these skills can be learned and put into practice. Once the basics have been mastered and templates made, further sets of covers can be made with the confidence of experience, and a first success will inspire you to ever more projects. But, loose covers are an investment and the making should not be taken lightly; neither in time, nor expense. Buying inexpensive fabrics is always false economy – for all the work which you will put into your covers, they should serve you well. With fabric you really do get the quality for which you pay.

Try to obtain information about the 'rub test' of any fabric which you intend to purchase. Most fabric companies rely on the Martindale test, in which a sample fabric is put into simulated normal use to clarify the extent of wear. A fabric rated 15,000 is only suitable for very occasional use covers whereas 60,000 would satisfy the most abused family sofa. A 35,000-40,000 classification will cover most general uses and will include many good quality furnishing fabrics. However, for a piece of furniture experiencing minimum wear, don't reject stunningly beautiful drapery fabrics because they are a low grading.

Natural fibres are comfortable to work with and to use. Cotton, whether fine lawn or heavy velvet, makes up and wears with impunity. Whether woven into stripes or checks, dobby weaves, towelling or damasks, knitted or printed, there are more loose cover fabrics available in cotton than can be imagined.

Linen union, which is a blend of cotton and linen fibres, is often hailed as the perfect loose cover fabric. It is good value for money, but in time the stronger threads cut into the weaker – rather as the harder of two gold rings will wear away the softer. One hundred per cent linen is the best to work with, easy to manipulate, and seams finger-press like a dream, but the best linen is costly. Plain and inexpensive linens will show every fault and crease; so test a piece first. Printed linens are the most forgiving and good tempered: perfect for professionals and beginners alike.

I hope the selection of armchairs, sofas, small chairs and stools shown within this book will inspire you to rummage through upholstery fabrics, and master the basic skills of loose cover making so that you can use my ideas to spark off your own.

BASIC TECHNIQUES

STITCHES

Always ensure you start and finish all stitching with a double stitch; never use a knot.

Herringbone stitch

Herringbone stitch is always used over any raw edge for lined covers or valances which have hand-stitched hems.

Ladder stitch

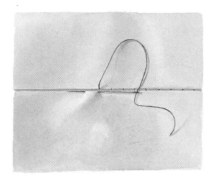

Ladder stitch is used to join two folded edges invisibly together. Slide the needle along the fold 5 mm (¼ in) and straight into the fold opposite. Slide along for 5 mm (¼ in) and back into the first fold, again directly opposite.

Slip stitch

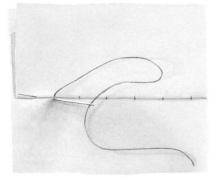

This is used for handsewing gussets and plackets. Make each stitch approximately 1.5 cm (⅝ in). Slide the needle through the fold by 1.5 cm (⅝ in) and pick up two threads of the opposite fabric. Push the needle back into the main fabric exactly opposite and slide through a further 1.5 cm (⅝ in).

Buttonhole stitch

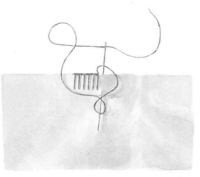

Used of course for buttonholes, but also wherever a raw edge needs to be strengthened or neatened. Work from left to right with the raw edge uppermost. Push the needle from the back to the front, approximately 3 mm (⅛ in) below the edge. Twist the thread around the needle and pull

the needle through, carefully tightening the thread so that it knots right on the edge of the fabric to form a ridge.

Blanket stitch

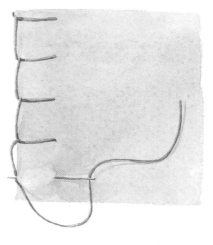

Originally used to neaten the raw edges of woollen blankets, its use is now mainly decorative. It is most comfortable worked from the side with the edge towards you. Push the needle from the front to the back, about 6 mm (¼ in) from the edge (this measurement will vary with large or small items). Hold the thread from the last stitch under the needle and pull up to make a loop on the edge.

Hemming stitch

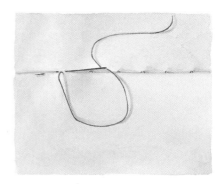

Used for hemming unlined covers, each stitch should be roughly

1.5 cm (⅝ in) in length. Slide the needle through the folded hem, pick up two threads of the main fabric, and push the needle directly back into the fold.

PINNING

When pinning two layers of fabric together or piping on to fabric, always use horizontal and vertical pins to keep the fabric in place from both directions. The horizontal pins need to be removed just before the machine foot reaches them and the vertical ones – or cross pins – can remain in place, so the fabrics are held together the whole time.

SEAMS

Flat seam

The most common and straight-forward seam for normal use. With right sides together, pin 1.5–2 cm (⅝–¾ in) in from the edges at 10 cm

(4 in) intervals. Pin cross pins halfway between each seam pin. These cross pins will remain in place while you are stitching to prevent the fabrics slipping. Once machine-stitched, open the seam flat and press from the back. Press from the front. Now press from the back, under each flap, to remove the pressed ridge line.

French seam

Use this seam for unlined fine cotton covers. Pin the fabrics together with the wrong sides facing. Stitch 5 mm (¼ in) from the raw edges. Trim and flip the fabric over, bringing the right sides together. Pin again, 1 cm (⅜ in) from the stitched edge and stitch along this line to enclose the raw edges. Press from the right side, always pressing the seam in one direction only.

Flat fell seam

Use for heavier weight fabrics. Pin the fabrics together with the right

sides facing and stitch 1.5–3 cm (⅝–1¼ in) from the raw edges. Trim one seam to just under half. Fold the other over to enclose the raw edge. Press down. Stitch close to the fold line.

MITRED CORNERS

For a neat and professional finish, you will need to mitre the hemmed corners of unlined covers and valances.

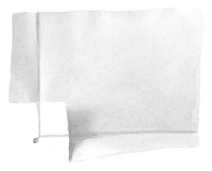

1. Press the side seam over and the hem up. Position a pin through the point of the corner.

2. Open out the folds and turn in the corner at a 45⁰ angle, with the pin at the centre of the fold line.

3. Fold the hem up and the sides in again along the original fold lines. Keep the pin on the point and make sure the fabric is firmly tucked into the folded lines.

MAKING TIES

Ties are useful and decorative and used extensively for soft furnishings, especially loose covers.

Folded ties

Cut a strip of fabric four times the width of your finished tie and 3 cm (1¼ in) longer.

Press one short end under by 1 cm (⅜ in). Press in half lengthwise, fold each side to the middle, press, fold and stitch close to the folded edges.

Rouleau ties

Cut a strip of fabric four times the width of your finished tie and 3 cm (1¼ in) longer. Fold in half lengthwise, right sides together, enclosing a piece of cord which is longer than the strip of fabric. Stitch along the short side to secure the cord firmly. If the rouleau is quite wide, knot the cord as well. Stitch along the length, 2 mm (⅛ in) towards the raw edge from the centre.

Trim the fabric across the corner, pull the cord through, at the same time turning the fabric right side out. Cut off the cord at the end. Press the raw edge under and slipstitch with small stitches.

PIPING

If piping is to be used in straight lines then it will be easier to cut it straight. If it is to be bent around corners, then it should be cut on the cross. For 4 mm (⅛ in) piping cord cut 4 cm (1½ in) wide strips. All joins should be made on the cross to minimise bulk when the fabric is folded.

To cut on the straight
Cut lengths as long as possible. Hold two strips, butting the ends together as if making a continuous length. Trim away both corners at a 45⁰ angle. Hold together and flip the top one over. Stitch where the two pieces cross.

To cut on the cross
With the fabric flat on the table, fold one bottom corner as if making a 30 cm (12 in) square. Cut along the fold line. Mark pencil lines from this cut edge at 4 cm (1½ in) intervals, and cut along these lines. Hold two pieces butting the ends together as if making a continuous strip. Flip the top one over and stitch together where the two fabrics cross.

Making up and pinning on

Press seams flat and cut away excess corners. Fold in half along the length and insert the piping cord. Machine stitch to encase, approximately 2 mm (⅛ in) from the cord. Keep the fabric folded exactly in half.

Always pin piping so that the raw edges of the piping line up with those of the main fabric.

To bend piping around curves, snip into the stitching line for the piping to lie flat. For a right angle, stop pinning 1.5 cm (⅝ in) from the corner, snip the piping right to the stitching line, fold the piping to 90⁰ and start pinning 1.5 cm (⅝ in) on the adjacent side.

Joining
To join piping, overlap by approximately 6 cm (2¼ in). Unpick the casing on one side and cut away the cord so that the two ends butt up. Fold the piping fabric across at a 45⁰ angle and cut along this fold. Fold under 1 cm (⅜ in) and then pin before stitching.

BINDING

Binding one edge
1. Cut the binding strips to the width required. Join the strips to

make the required length.
2. Pin the binding to the fabric, right sides together and stitch 1.4 cm (slightly less than ⅝ in) from the raw edges.

3. Neaten the raw edges to 1.4 cm (slightly less than ⅝ in). Press from the front, pressing the binding away from the main fabric. Fold the binding to the back, measuring the edge to 1.5 cm (⅝ in), keeping the fabric tucked firmly into the fold and then pin at 8 cm (3¼ in) intervals. Turn to the back of the fabric and herringbone the edge of the binding to the main fabric.

Binding a corner

Stop pinning short of the corner by the width of the finished binding. Fold binding back on itself to make a sharp angle and pin across this fold line. Pin on the adjacent side, the same distance from the edge. Stitch binding on, stopping at the pin, and secure. Begin stitching again at the same point on the adjacent side. Press to mitre. Fold fabric to the back, mitring in the opposite direction.

PLACKET WITH TIES

1. Cut two pieces of fabric one 8 cm (3¼ in) and one 12 cm (4¾ in) wide, and each the length of the opening. Stitch the widest one to the back and the narrower one to the side of the chair cover, along the 2 cm (¾ in) seam allowance.

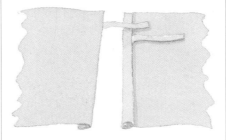

2. Starting with the back, press this wider flap forwards. Measure 3 cm (1¼ in) from the seam line and fold under. Turn over to the back, and fold under another 3 cm (1¼ in) so that the fold lines up with the stitching line on the back and pin. Press the side flap to the back and fold in half to make a hem.

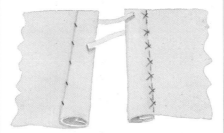

3. Finish the hemline, whether a valance will be attached, a binding or a self hem. Slip stitch along the

folded lines with small stitches.
   Pin the ties in place and insert with the first seam line. Add hooks and bars if you prefer.

INSERTING A ZIP

The first method is very straight-forward. The second is used for inserting a zip into a piped seam.

Method 1
1. Pin one side of the zip to the opening, 2 mm (⅛ in) away from the teeth. Machine topstitch this half of the zip in place.
2. Machine the other side of the opening to the zip, forming a flap to encase the teeth.

Method 2
1. Apply piping to the front of the fabric. Join front and back pieces together, allowing a gap for zip.

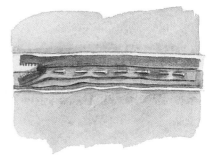

2. Pin one side of the zip against the piping line on the front of the cushion from the wrong side. Machine stitch tightly in place.
3. Open out cushion seam and pin other side of the zip in place, ensuring that the fabric butts up to the piping without gaping. Machine stitch in place, stitching across ends of zip to prevent the head becoming lost.

PREPARATION

This is the key to successful sewing. Prepare well, and the work should go smoothly, with few errors. Look at various factors before you begin: where you are going to work, what you plan to use, linings and interlinings. Here are some guidelines to bear in mind before you begin sewing.

For making loose covers you will need:

Main fabric – as plan
Calico to make a 'toile' or pattern
Long-bladed, sharp scissors for cutting
Short, sharp scissors for snipping
Long pins
Metre (yard) rule
Tape measure
Piping cord
12 mm (½ in) tape
Hooks for closure
Pins and needles

THE WORKTABLE

If possible, you should stake your claim on one room which can be put aside for your own use, even if it is only while you are making your covers.

A dining room or guest bedroom can be made into a temporary workroom with little effort. A worktable which is at least 2.5 x 1.2 m (8 x 4 ft) and preferably 3 x 1.5 m (10 x 5 ft) will make the whole job so much easier. You can buy a sheet of board in either of these sizes. Cover your dining table with thick felt so that the board can be rested safely on top.

Alternatively, make some sturdy legs which can be bracketed on to the underside of the board. This quickly made table can then be fitted temporarily over a guest bed. The space below can be used to store all your fabrics, and the top will be wide enough for you to work on a whole width of fabric at a time. Pure luxury compared to hands and knees on the floor! The height of the worktable should be whatever is comfortable for you; I use a table that is 95 cm (38 in) high.

Cover the top with heavy inter-lining and then a layer of lining. Staple these to the underside; pulling the fabrics very taut as you go. You will now have a soft surface which is ideal for pinning and pressing.

CHECKING THE FABRIC

Before you begin to cut the fabric, check it thoroughly for flaws or incorporate them into parts that will not be seen, such as hems. If the fabric is badly flawed, return it.

Measure out each length and mark with pins to make sure that you have the correct amount of fabric. Always double check your measurements before cutting.

Fabric should ideally be cut along the grain and to pattern, but sometimes the printing method allows the pattern to move off grain. If necessary, allow the pattern to run out slightly to either side – but a 2 cm (¾ in) run-off is the most you should tolerate.

PATTERN MATCHING

It is well worth spending a little time to make sure that all fabric patterns are matched correctly at the seam on each width.

1. Place one of the lengths of fabric right side up on the worktable with the selvedge facing you. Place the next length over the first, right side down. Fold over the selvedge to reveal roughly 5 mm (¼ in) of pattern and press lightly.

2. Match the pattern to the piece underneath, and pin through the fold line along the whole length. You may need to ease one of the sides at times – using more pins will help. Go back and place cross pins between each pin. Machine or hand stitch along the fold line, removing the straight pins and stitching over the cross pins.

3. Press the seam from the wrong side and then again from the front. Use a hot iron and press quickly. Turn the fabric over again to the back and press under the seam to remove the pressed ridges. If the background fabric is dark or you are using a woven fabric, snip into the selvedges at 5 cm (2 in) intervals. If the background fabric is light, trim the selvedges back to 1.5 cm (⅝ in), removing any printed writing.

PLACING THE PATTERN

The pattern should be placed so that it always runs from top to bottom. For this reason the outside and inside arm pieces should never be cut as one. Patterns should run from the top of the inside arm to the seat and from the top of the outside arm towards the floor. Match all patterned or geometrc prints at each piping seam. Plan all pieces so that the pattern follows up through from the floor, across the seat and up the back.

CUSHION PATTERNS

Cushions should always be made to match the position of the pattern on the main body of the sofa or chair cover. If possible, plan enough fabric to make all cushions reversible.

If you have made a paper template of the chair seat or stool, transfer this to calico or scrap fabric and add 2 cm (¾ in) all round for seams. If the cushions are square or rectangular, measure carefully and note the longest and widest measurements. Add 2 cm (¾ in) all round for seam allowances. Measure gussets, frills, piping and note the sizes needed, adding seam allowances.

Plan these pieces (top, bottom, gusset, etc) on the worktable to see how they fit into the fabric width. If you are making several matching cushions, they must be planned thoughtfully to obtain maximum benefit from the fabric.

If the fabric has a dominant pattern, the pieces will need to be planned thoughtfully so that the cushions are cut together to prevent wastage of fabric.

On seat and back cushions, patterns should always read from front to back. The gusset should be placed so that the pattern follows through and matches exactly. Piping may be cut on the cross or on the straight; if there are any curves or curved corners, cut on the cross so that the piping can be bent and still lie flat.

As a general rule, allow 1 m (1 yd) of fabric for each seat. So allow approximately 2 m (2 ¼ yd) for a two-seat sofa.

Also allow for pattern repeats. Small geometric patterns and all-over designs need approximately 10 per cent extra fabric; large prints may need almost double the amount a plain fabric will take to match up correctly. Fabric bindings need to be of similar weight to the main fabric, or instead try wide ribbon, linen tape or upholstery webbing.

PLANNING FABRIC CUTS

Look at the chair or sofa you wish to cover and try to visualise it finished. Decide whether you prefer a plain or patterned fabric; whether a print or weave, whether the pattern should be large or small; where the piping lines should be; whether you want to define a particular line or 'lose' another; whether the piping should be toning, contrasting, or as the main fabric; how formal the chair will be; whether the valance should be frilled, box pleated, corner pleated, fringed, etc.

View the chair as a series of rectangles, i.e. inside back; outside back; inside arm; outside arm; seat; front gusset; valance; cushion pieces; armcover. Measure the chair for each piece, allowing 3–4 cm (1¼–1½ in) seam allowance in each direction, plus 10–20 cm (4–8 in) for 'tuck-in'. Push your hand down into the chair around the seat, the inside arm and inside the wing to check the depth.

The tuck-in should be as large as the space allows, as the further the fabric can be pushed in the less likely it is to pull out.

Seams should never be in the centre of a cover. Always use a full fabric width at the centre with panels joined at either side. Seams should follow from the front, across the seat and up through the back.

PIPING

Piping cord is available commercially in a wide range of thicknesses, graded numerically according to the diameter of the cord, corresponding roughly to the metric measurement of the diameter. Therefore a 5 mm (¼ in) diameter cord is designated No. 5. No. 00 is the narrowest cord and No. 7 is the widest one that is normally available.

Piping strips should be cut to make a 2 cm (¾ in) seam after the fabric has been folded around the cord. 5 cm (2 in) strips will fit No. 4 cord, which is the most generally used size.

Tiny pipings are used for decorative work and in places where piping is desirable but a thick edge of colour is not. Chunky piping cords are used where a statement is needed and can be very effective if self piping, so that the size rather than a contrast colour makes the detail.

MEASURING AND PLANNING

ESTIMATING FOR AN ARMCHAIR

Plan your pieces (see right) on to paper to make best use of the fabric width to estimate the amount needed. With a patterned fabric, it is best to mark the paper into sections to show the repeat and the pattern size. Cushions should be planned so that backs and fronts are the same and that each one is reversible or reversible with each other. The shape of the sofa or chair will dictate the reversibility of cushions.

DINING OR SIDE CHAIR

Measure the chair at the widest and highest points, following this list as a guide.

Inside back   – width
      – length + tuck in
Outside back – width
      – length to floor or top of skirt
Seat   – front width
      – back width
      – front to back + tuck-in
Skirt   – to floor
      – all around
Add 6 cm (2¼ in) all around for seam allowances. Allow 15 cm (6 in) for the tuck-in at the back of the seat, and 20 cm (8 in) for the

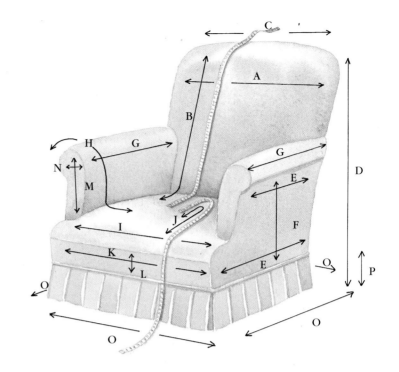

Pieces to measure

Inside back	A – width		H – length over arm + tuck-in
	B – length+ tuck-in		
Outside back	C – width	Seat	I – width + tuck-in
	D – length to valance or floor		J – length + tuck-in
		Front gusset	K – width
Outside arm	E – width, measure top and bottom		L – depth
		Front arm	M – height
	F – depth		N – width
Inside arm	G – width, measure top and bottom	Sides	O – around the frame
		Valance	P – depth of valance

Direction of pattern

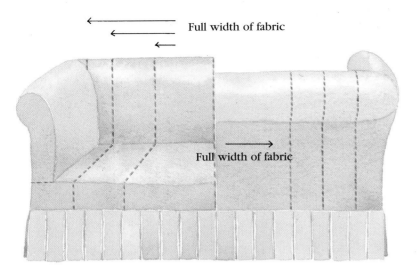

Full width of fabric

Full width of fabric

Seam positions

this purpose, I prefer newspaper, which is soft enough to fold and tear easily to fit around difficult leg and arm interruptions. A thick pencil is useful to mark the edges of the seat on to the paper, and sticky tape will help hold the folds and tears in place. I then transfer this pattern to heavier brown paper from which I cut the fabric and pad patterns.

flap under the chair seat. Decide whether you want to have a valance around the chair seat, and if so, the style and fullness. Also consider whether to have any other decoration.

Plan these pieces on to graph paper to calculate the fabric needed. Make allowance for any pattern repeat and choose the pattern position on the chair back and seat.

CUTTING OUT

Cut out the pieces of fabric as planned. Use calico if you are making a toile or straight into the top cover if you are confident. Make up enough piping cord for the whole job.

Using the tape measure, place a vertical row of pins to mark the centre line of the inside back, outside back, front and seat.

WOODEN CHAIRS

Squab cushions add a decorative, welcoming touch to a wooden

chair seat, but the primary function is to make a hard chair seat more comfortable. Foam or rubberised hair with a wadding wrap are the best padding solutions for this type of cushion.

You will need to cut a template from the actual chair seat to use as an accurate pattern for the seat shapes. Either paper, or tightly woven cotton are suitable, but for

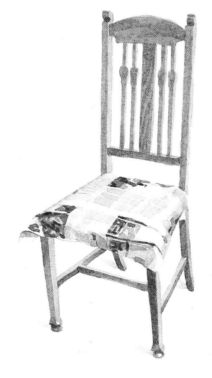

Tape paper to the back, front and sides of the chair seat. Bend the paper along the shaped seat and confirm the line with a thick pencil. Tear and fold the paper around the arms and legs to give you a really accurate shape. Remember, you can always stick a bit of paper back on if you over-cut by accident. The important thing is to fit the paper surely enough to gain an accurate template from which to cut your final pattern.

TAILORED COVERS

Good use was made of the printed fabric border. Instead of a skirt, flaps stitched to the border fabric between each leg have been tucked underneath and tied at each corner.

Loose covers are an investment in time – firstly yours to make, then followed by years of use by family and friends. If you are a keen beginner I would advise you to start your loose cover career with a cover for a stool, bedroom, kitchen or garden chair. The worn-out sofa in the sitting room might be your reason for starting on this road, but there are some useful principles to learn which might be less painful on a smaller subject, with less fabric at risk.

Of course, once you become really competent, you will have to hide your new-found light under the nearest bushel, or your services will be in great demand! Everyone wants to know a loose cover maker.

You will need to decide how 'tight' or 'loose' your loose cover should be. The best tight covers are hardly recognisable as loose covers, fitting so snugly over upholstery that not a wrinkle can be seen. Excellent for formal-style sofas and chairs and traditional rooms, tight covers look upholstered but may be removed easily for laundering. Very baggy covers – slip covers usually in light cotton or calico – were originally dust covers but are now highly fashionable as summer overalls for sofas and wooden side chairs alike.

Loose covers are normally easier to make if they are fitted tightly but made up with some easement – so that a wobbly seam or an uneven cut is disguised. Overall patterns are sympathetic, disguising odd creases, whereas plain fabrics will show all discrepancies. Choose carefully to make life as easy as possible.

CUTTING THE COVER

Refer to pages 10-13 before you begin in earnest and practise with a toile if you are nervous. Loose covers must always be fitted with the fabric pinned in place right side out, i.e. as it will look when finished. This is because not only are there never two chairs exactly the same, neither are the left and right sides of any one chair exactly the same!

1. Fold the inside back piece in half lengthwise, with the right sides of the fabric together. Finger press lightly. Line the fold line against the centre line of the chair and pin at top and bottom. Open out the piece and pin at 10–20 cm (4–8 in) intervals to anchor to the side and top of the chair. Pins should be at right angles to the chair with the points inwards. Repeat with the outside back, anchoring it to the sides and bottom of the chair frame as well.

2. Holding the fabric firmly between finger and thumb, pin the pieces together along the back edge of the chair. Remember that the pin line will be the seam/ piping line. Pins should be in a straight line, nose to tail, right against the furniture to give an accurate line for stitching later. Start and finish 4–6 cm (1½–2¼ in) above the arm on both sides. Pin from the back of the chair, and ease the front piece around shaped backs, making darts or small tucks at the corners.

3. Position the inside and outside arm pieces of one arm on to the chair, checking the pattern is in the right place, and keeping the grain straight, vertically and horizontally. The pattern and grain of the outside arm should be level with the floor not the top of the arm.

Pin these pieces together along the arm, making some allowance for any arm curvature. The seam may be at the top of the arm, on the outside of the arm or under the scroll, depending on the actual arm style of the chair. Repeat with the other arm.

4. Pin the arm fronts to the chair, checking that the grain is straight. Fix the position with two crossed pins. Anchor all around, with pins at right angles to the chair, points inwards.

5. Pin the inside and outside arm pieces to the arm front, easing curves and fullness. Some arms will have no fullness to disperse, other arms will need one or two darts at this point, but mostly the excess fabric will be eased in with small gathers or pleats, spread evenly around the curved section.

6. Pin the outside arm pieces to the chair back piece. Joining the back arm to the inner back is the trickiest part so should be practised with spare calico if you are a beginner. If you over-cut the seam, the cover will be too tight and if you under-cut, too loose. Fold the inside back piece up so that the fold line marks the seam from the top of the arm to the back. Fold the arm piece to make the opposite side of the seam.

7. Cut away the excess fabric to 3–4 cm (1¼–1½ in) seam allowance as far as the start of the curve of the arm and the seat back (do not cut this too tightly yet in case some adjustment is needed). Make marking tacks with contrast thread three or four times along the folds at exactly opposite points so that the pieces can be matched accurately for seaming.

8. Pencil a line around the arm curve and down into the seat. Trim 3 cm (1¼ in) away from this pencil line where there is no tuck-in space and approximately 10 cm (4 in) where there is. Do the same with the inner arm. Either pin the fabrics together along the pencilled line or fold each back on themselves. The actual shape of the arm and the extent of the curve will make one of these methods easier than the other. Snip right into the seam allowances where necessary for the fabric to lie flat. Gradually cut the seam allowance back to 2 cm (¾ in).

9. Trim the whole cover, leaving a 2 cm (¾ in) seam allowance all around. Cut V-shaped balance marks so that the pieces can be easily matched for stitching.

10. Stitch individual tailor tacks in contrasting thread to each piece at the actual meeting point of the arm seam with the arm front, and at any other area where they might be useful for matching the pieces before stitching. Repeat with the other arm.

11. Place the seat piece on to the chair seat, again matching the centre fold to the pinned line, and anchor all around.

12. Fold the two sides over along the length of the arms, so that the fold lines join the arm fronts at the edge of the front of the chair. Pin the front gusset to the front of the chair, checking that it is centred and level with the floor. Pin the top of this piece to the seat piece along the front edge. Where these two pieces meet the arm front, push a pin through all three pieces so that there is a definite point at which all pieces will meet when stitched. Mark each piece individually with a secure tack in contrast thread at this point.

13. Pin the front gusset to the arm fronts, from the marked join to the bottom of both pieces. Measure and mark the folded back sides of the seat piece so that the tuck-in is equal from front to back along the length of the arm. Cut carefully along this line.

14. Pin the inside arm pieces to the seat piece for approximately 20 cm (8 in) from the front towards the back, cutting back and shaping the join to correspond with the available tuck-in allowance.

15. Using a wooden ruler, measure up from the floor all around to the skirt position. Mark with pins. Allow for the seam allowance and cut the excess fabric away. At this point, if the chair needs to have a back opening, fold back the outside arm piece and the back piece to allow the necessary easement. Pin the fabric back on itself to keep the fold. Mark the top of the opening with a tack on each piece.

16. Tidy up and cut all seam allowances so that they are equal. (If you have accidentally under-cut at any point, mark the place, so that you can adjust the seam allowance to compensate when pinning the pieces, together.) Make sure that you have snipped enough balance marks. Use single, double and triple cuts to make matching easier. Remove the anchor pins and lift the cover off.

MAKING UP

If you want the cover to be loose, you will need to stitch so that the seam allowance is less than that allowed, i.e. a stitched seam allowance of 1.5 cm (⅝ in) of the 2 cm (¾ in) allowed in cutting will give 5 mm (¼ in) easement on each side of the seam. It is usual to pin the piping so that the front of the cord is on the seam allowance to give some easement.

The instructions have been given for a 'tight' cover with the stitching line of the piping pinned along the seam allowance.

Make your own adjustments as you prefer, keeping them consistent throughout the making up. Always work with small areas at a time so that there is a limited amount of the unstitched cover unpinned at any one time.

1. Take the pins from one of the seams joining the inside arm to the back. These seams are probably the most vulnerable to movement and fraying so should be stitched and secured first. Turn inside out. Starting at the back, carefully match the tacks, and the ends of the easement cuts. Pin the seam down to the seat. Stitch, reinforcing the curve line by stitching two rows very close together. Do not be afraid to stitch right next to the cuts. If you give these too much berth the cover will not fit back as well as it came off. Neaten the seam. Repeat with the other side.

2. Next unpin one of the arm seams. If piping is to be used on the seam, pin the piping to the right side of the outside arm piece. Stitch in place. Pin the inside arm to the piping line, right sides together, so that the seam allowances and notches match. Stitch. Pin along the piping line and at right angles to it. The pins along the piping must be removed as the machine approaches, but the others can remain in place, preventing the two layers of fabric 'walking'. Stitch in place as close to the piping as possible. Check from the front that the previous stitching line is not visible.

If you have used piping, pull the cord from inside the case at each end for 2 cm (¾ in). Cut the cord away so that the casing lies flat beyond the point at which the back and arm front seam will cross. Neaten the seam. Repeat with the other arm.

3. Unpin the front gusset. Turn inside out, pin the piping along the gusset piece and stitch. At the join with the arm front, pull the cord from the piping case 2 cm (¾ in). Cut away the cord so that the case is flat beyond the tack mark. Pin the right side of the seat piece to the piping line, matching seam allowance and notches. Stitch the length of the piping, between the tack marks. Secure stitches firmly at each end. Neaten this seam.

4. Unpin the sides of the seat from front to back. Turn inside out and pin together again, matching notches and seam allowance. Stitch from the front tack mark to the seam at the back.

5. Unpin one of the front arms. Turn inside out. Pin piping all around the arm, to the right side of the fabric, snipping piping at 1 cm (¾ in) intervals to ease around any curve. Make sure that you have pinned the piping to give a good shape, and stitch. Pin the inside arm, outside arm and the front gusset to the arm front, matching seam allowances and balance marks. Pin the arm seam so that it is pressed downwards.

6. Ease any fullness carefully. Stitch from the bottom of the front gusset up to the join with the seat. Finish with the needle in the tack mark. Secure with backward and forward stitches to this point. Lift the cover away from the machine. Fold over the seam and start again, with the needle in the tack mark from the other side of the seam.

7. Stitch all around. Look at the stitching line from the front. You might find it quite hard to get close to the piping the first time, because of the joint difficulties of the curve and the fullness. Stitching a small section at a time, slowly stitch as close to the piping as you can, so that the previous stitching line is not visible from the front. Neaten the seam. Repeat with other arm. Ease one fabric on to the other. Shown above is the scroll arm.

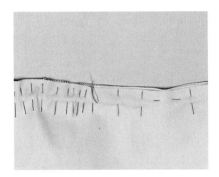

8. Repeat the same stitching process on the centre back, remembering to stitch just a small amount at a time.

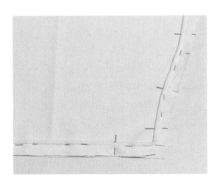

9. Unpin the back piece. Pin the piping to the right side of the fabric from just above each arm. Snip to ease where necessary and stitch in place.

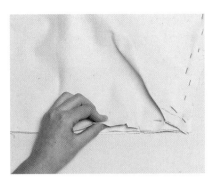

10. Pin the front to the back piece along the piping line. Use plenty of pins, pinned at right angles to the piping to ease any fullness. At the top corners make sure that the hand-stitched or darted corners lie flat and that the finishing off stitches are inside the seam allowance. Stitch as close to the piping as possible.

11. Sleeve the cover back on to the chair. Check that the seam lines are good and re-stitch any that aren't satisfactory.

12. Check that the hemline is still straight and an even distance from the floor. Make the back opening placket if needed (see page 9). Make up a valance or skirt and stitch to the hemline. Stitch the end of the placket to enclose the raw edges at the end of the valance. Fix hooks and bars or ties (see page 9).

13. Press all seams from the front over a damp cloth. Press out the cover and ease back on to the chair. Make sure that the seams all lie in the same direction. Ease the cover around curves and corners. Finger press piping lines to straighten. You will need to spend time easing and fitting the cover into place to obtain the best fit.

Loose covers transform a dining room chair: This bright check can be removed and cleaned easily.

VALANCES

Although not essential, skirts or valances are most useful both to disguise poor legs and to alter the visual impact of a chair or sofa. In a room full of leggy side chairs and tables, valances on one or two chairs or a single sofa can redress the balance and make the situation immediately more pleasing. This country-style chair with its distressed, blue-painted legs has been given a more comfortable appearance by the addition of a gently frilled printed linen valance. Always make up the valance separately and attach to the otherwise finished cover.

MAKING UP

Decide the depth you wish the valance to be. Add seam allowances of 2 cm (¾ in) for the top and 6 cm (2¼ in) for the hem. Measure the sides, front and back of the chair separately. Plan your valance to fit the four sides. Corner-pleated valances are arguably the most used, the simplest to make and ideal for formal situations.

Corner-pleated valance

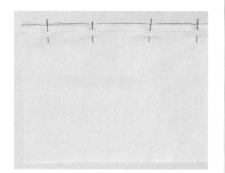

1. Add 40 cm (15¾ in) for the pleats at each corner. Allow 3.5 cm (1⅜ in) to one back piece for the underlap if there is a back opening. Plan to cut each section so that there are no visible seams. Sofa valances will need to have seams either side of the central width on the front and back sections, following those on the seat and outer back seams. It should be possible to hide all other seams inside the pleats at each corner.

Cut the lining to match. Seam the short sides and press flat. Stitch the lining and top fabric together along the length, 1.5 cm (⅝ in) from the lower edge.

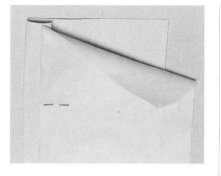

2. Press the seam towards the lining so that fabric bulk is kept to a minimum. Press the main fabric over to the lining side by 3 cm (1¼ in). Pin together and press lightly from the front.

3. Handstitch the short ends. On the right side, measure and mark out each side and each pleat. Pin pleats in position and tack to hold. Pin piping along the top edge. Stitch. Pull the cord away at each end and fold the raw ends inwards.

4. Stitch the valance to the chair cover. If there is a back opening on the cover, first neaten the raw ends at the top of the underlap by carefully slip stitching the bottom of the placket over.

Frilled valance

1. Add measurements of the four chair sides together and multiply by fullness required - usually two to two-and-a-half times. Add 5 cm (2 in) for any underlap at the back. Divide figure by the fabric width, and cut widths required for this length. Cut lining the same depth and enough widths for same length.

2. Join seams and press flat. Pin main fabric and lining together along one long side. Stitch 1.5 cm (⅝ in) from edge. Press hem 4 cm (1½ in) to back. Pin together along top edge. Stitch a gathering thread 1.5 cm (⅝ in) down. Divide length of valance into eight and mark each section with a marking tack. Divide cover hem into eight sections and mark. Match marking tacks and ease gathers evenly. Stitch close to piping - two rows are probably needed to come close enough to cover first stitching line.

Binding the hem

1. Cut fabric strips four times the finished binding width, e.g. 6 cm (2½ in) wide for a 1.5 cm (⅝ in) bound edge. Cut valance and lining fabrics plus 1.5 cm (⅝ in) for a top seam allowance but not at bottom. Stitch lining to one long side and valance fabric to the other, 1.35 cm (just over ½ in) from raw edges. Press both seams towards binding, and from front to remove puckers.

2. Fold binding in half and press. Pin top of both fabrics together.

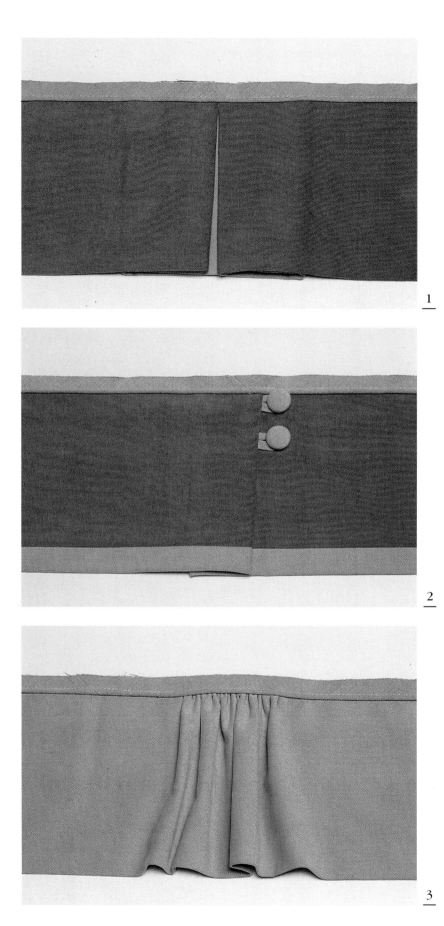

1

2

3

SKIRT SELECTION

When the sofa or chair has been piped with an alternative fabric, whether a contrasting colour, say blue and white, or a toning contrast such as deep pink on soft pink, or a complementary fabric such as a small check on a floral print, the same theme will continue to the skirt. Perhaps just one row of piping at the top will be all that is needed, but binding the hem serves to 'weight' the skirt. Buttons with loops or buttonholes, poppers, ties, frogging and many other dressmaking finishes can be used to decorate the corners of the skirts, as long as the method allows each skirt section to remain sharp at each corner.

Binding the hem might have a more practical use when, for example, the main fabric has a rose print on a light ground and the piping fabric is a deeper tone, as the deeper edge disguises dirt picked up from the floor.

1. Contrast piping and inset pleats smarten up a simple corner-pleated valance/skirt.
2. Each valance/skirt section is made up separately with the sides cut 10 cm (4 in) longer at the front and back so that these sections can overlap. Make rouleau loops and stitch at the end of the valance between the top fabric and the lining. The contrast edgings and details are optional and, depending on the room style, can be sharply contrasting or gently toning.
3. Cut the valance in one long

length, adding approximately
16 cm (6¼ in) to gather around
each corner – this is a softer alternative to a pleat.

4. A frilled valance gives a soft
and homely finish to a country-
style or casual sofa. Contrast
binding and piping are not
necessary but can make all the
difference. Choose mid-toned,
plain colours to go with patterned
fabrics, a small print or stripe with
a larger all-over print, or closely
toned plain colours.

5. Knife-pleated skirts fill the gap
between the informal, feminine
frilled valance and the formal,
masculine straight skirt. Allow
three times the fullness and make
each pleat so that it starts right
where the last finished. They are
approximately 4 cm (1½ in) wide.
Plan them to fit exactly between
two chair corners. This means that
the pleat sizes might vary slightly
on each side but this should not
be at all noticeable.

6. Box pleats are made in the
same manner as knife pleats.
Allow three times fullness, pleat
each one against the next and
divide equally between the sides
so that a chair corner always fits at
the centre of a pleat.

   Box pleats, knife pleats,
inverted pleats and tapered pleats
are traditional skirt finishes for
both formal and informal
situations. Formal rooms and
severe furniture will require fewer,
very tailored pleats; cottage style
furniture needs pleating to be
informal, so smaller pleats which
kick out playfully rather than
standing side by side in strict
rows, are probably preferable.

4

5

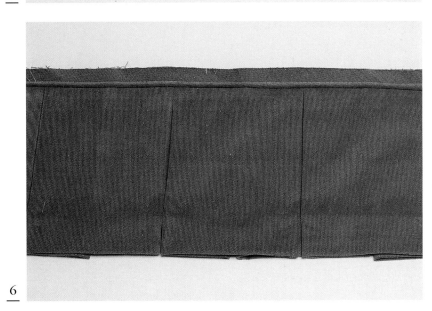

6

DESIGN AND MAKE LOOSE COVERS

ARM SHAPES

It is rare to find two arms that are exactly the same size on an old armchair or sofa, and it is also often the case on a new one. Small differences on new arms are not easy to spot, but still each arm will need to be cut out separately.

The rounded club arm extending to a slight 'wing' (left) shows one of the many and varied arm and side combinations which you might find. The importance of good straight piping lines, evenly spaced, is apparent.

Old arms will misshapen with use over the years and almost always one arm has been flattened more than the other. Small upholstery repairs might be needed – a little re-padding and tightening of the top cover, for example – but much can be disguised by a well-thought-out and fitted loose cover.

Your priority must be to keep the piping lines that run the length of the arm very straight and positioned in the best place. It is difficult to give much direction on this because there are so many arm shapes. On a scroll arm, the seam could be almost at the top or right on the side (see below); on a club arm the seam should give a clear edge, and on a laid back arm the seam could be along the most prominent edge or tucked down into the outside roll. Pin the two arm pieces together in several positions or alternatively draw pencil lines along the arm to help you visualise.

THE STRAIGHT ARM

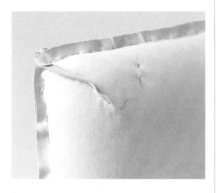

The traditional straight arm or Victorian 'laid back' arm can both be treated in this way. A pinned and stitched dart is the preferred finish for a sharp corner, but if the arm is more rounded than this one, then controlled pleats can be a most attractive way to ease the fullness of the inside arm piece.

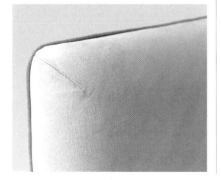

THE CLUB ARM

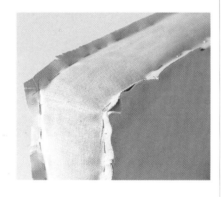

The club arm needs to have its form identified with very straight piping lines. The distance between the piping lines on the front arm and along the top arm must be measured accurately so that the gusset takes priority in the fitting. Any lumps and bumps must be taken up in the side panels.

THE SCROLL ARM

Scroll arms can be fat or thin, short or tall, squidgy or firm. Use your eye to make a good front shape and allow the front piece to take priority in the fitting. To make a misshapen arm beautiful, stitch piping on to the front arm piece first and then pin the sides to the defined line.

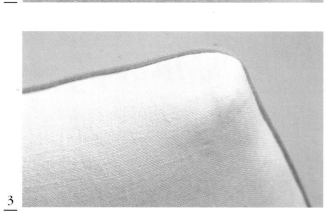

1

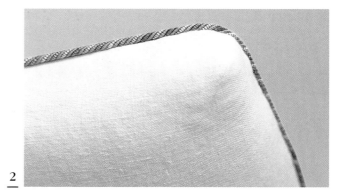

3

5

2

4

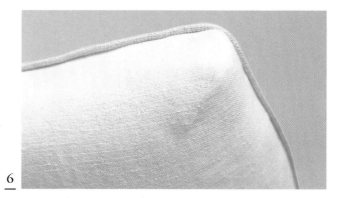

6

FINISHING DETAILS

The decision whether to define the edges and outline of the sofa or chair or not is personal choice. Piping in some form is needed to give definition and to aid stitching, but self piping is quite enough if there is no need for any other decoration. Flat piping, cording, ruched braid, small pleats or a tiny frilled edge are all plausible alter-

natives for varying situations and fabric choices. For instance, velvet piping is difficult for a beginner to sew, so cording or ruching should be chosen.

1. Self piping gently defines the shape of the sofa or chair without making a conscious statement.

2. Cording might be flanged for stitching into, with the seam as fabric piping, or stitched in place afterwards with a circular needle.

3. A plain contrast should be soft in tone if the room is subtlely

decorated, but it can be a dramatic contrast in a bold room.

4. Large and small checks give a 'now you see me now you don't' compromise between self piping and toned contrast.

5. Flat 'piping' uses the same piping strips but no cord. This is ideal for cushions in wicker or Lloyd Loom chairs.

6. Chunky piping in the same colour and fabric, or of another texture, can make a statement on structured furniture.

ARM COVERS

Arm covers are large affairs extending the length of the arm and long enough at each side to tuck right down behind the seat cushion and into the sofa, and to finish along the top of the valance on the outside. This arm cover was truly invisible as the stripes of sofa and arm cover match perfectly. We had to push the arm cover to one side and position the camera carefully to be able to show how the bottom of the arm has been cut away to match the upholstery beneath.

Armcaps are shorter than the length of the arm and, although the inside will still tuck down beside the cushion, the outside will be cut away to finish along the arm approximately 10-15 cm (4-6 in) down. On a scroll arm, the arm cover will be cut to snuggle into the recess.

ARM FINISHES

Slip-over covers or informal loose covers are more fashion orientated and therefore provide more opportunity for decorative finishes and different shapes than tailored covers. These four ideas were cut on a scroll arm, but can be adapted to a club, straight, wing or laid back arm. With a T-shape cushion, the front skirt will need to return along the side to join the front panel.

1. Both the side and front fall straight to the floor. Contrasting fabric piping, a let-in flap and covered button bring attention to the detail.

2. Self-piped seams allow the decorative buttons to take the attention. Rouleau loops, character buttons, elaborate frogging, ribbons or toggles are some other ideas for a decorative 'closure'.

3. Unpiped seams are perfect for the simplest, relaxed slip-over summer cover. Rouleau ties casually control the inset panel and outside edge. Stitch in place firmly to prevent restless fingers destroying your creation.

4. Stitch a series of small contrast ties to the outside edge and create a row of neatly tied bows to bring a touch of formality.

Top: A junk shop find, this simple kitchen chair becomes attractive and intensely practical with its new slip cover. Above: Accurate pattern matching is essential for a professional finish as are hand sewn cotton bars for small restraining hooks.

Always cut arm covers with the finished cover on the chair so that accurate allowances for piping and exact pattern matching can be achieved. Plan, cut and fit in the same way as you did to make the main cover. Full-sized arm covers are slip stitched to the back piping, seam, or opening, becoming virtually indistinguishable as separate pieces.

For cleaning, just unpick the stitches, launder and re-stitch when almost dry. Armcaps are held in position with small stitched touch-and-close fasteners, hooks and stitched bars, or loose cover pins.

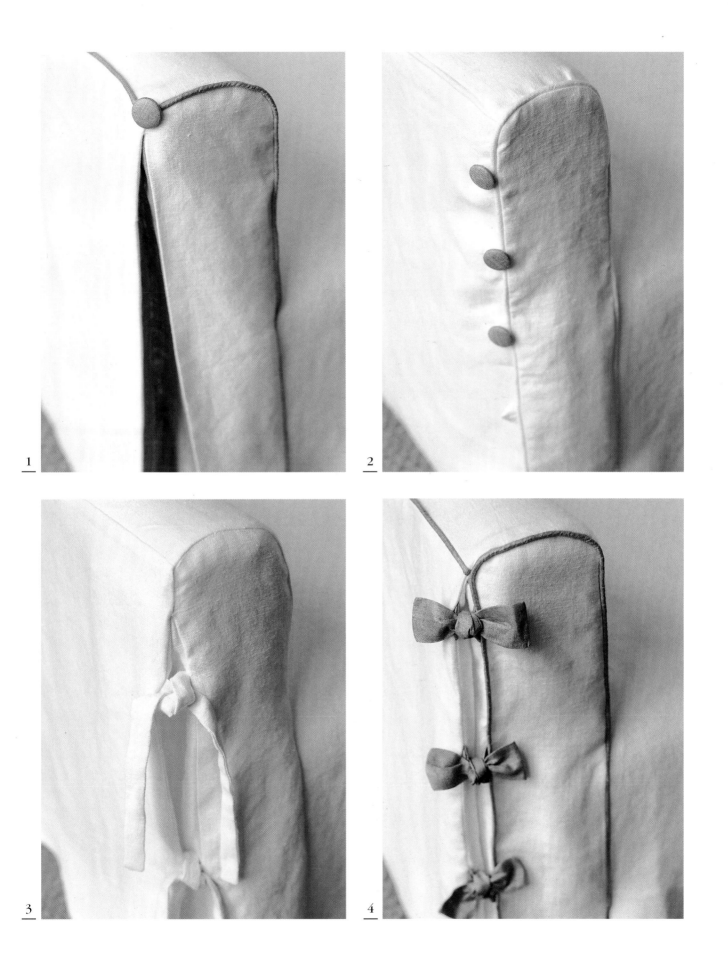

WINGS

The wing of an armchair or sofa, however small, usually needs to be cut quite separately from the rest of the cover.

1. Cut out pieces for the backs and arms as before. Pin the inner and outer chair backs together along the top of the chair. Pin each piece securely to the upholstery beneath. Cut and fit the arms.

2. For each wing, cut two squares, one for the inner and one for the outer side. Measure carefully – the distance between the back and front of the inner wing can be deceptive.

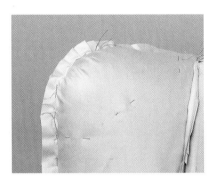

3. Pin each piece securely to the upholstery beneath, taking care to keep the grain straight. Use enough pins so that the centre line remains straight when pulled from both sides. Pin the pieces together around the front shaped edge, easing and snipping as necessary to make a good tight fit. Pin the length of the outside wing to the outside back.

4. Pin the inner wing and chair front pieces together at the top, making cuts and folding seam allowances as needed for the fabric to lie flat. Some wing chairs need the seam to angle back to the corner, but most will run straight from the point of tuck-in to 2–3 cm (¾–1¼ in) from the outside corner.

5. Push your hands into the tuck-in gap (the space between the wing and the inside back) to see how deep it is and where to start and stop the tuck-in.

Left: A loose cover extends the invitation to sit comfortably in this substantial wing chair, which underneath is upholstered in a rather strict manner.

Above: Rather than a separate wing, a chair might have a 'winged' side. Often, as here, the outer side is cut in one piece but the inner side will be cut in two pieces: one for the inside arm and one for the inside wing.

Pinning these together along the arm length allows any shaping and easing to be incorporated into a seam which can then be piped for strength.

QUILTING

Straight skirts were desirable but would have been too formal for this room. To present a relaxed atmosphere, the covers were cut overlong and both skirts and boxed cushions lightly quilted. Toned piping adds definition without calling immediate attention.

Quilting has often been called upon to save the day if a fabric is prone to creasing with constant use. Often employed for bedcovers and sofa and chair cushions, quilting gives a 'natural' creased effect which is much more attractive than the creasing which often occurs across cotton covers. Quilting can be used to create form, as geometric designs are imposed on a plain fabric, or 'outline' quilting can identify a particular pattern.

Always cut fabric to be quilted 3–10 per cent larger. Light quilting through one layer of curtain interlining or 50 g (2 oz) polyester wadding would need only 3 per cent overcut. If you want to promote a design, then up to three layers of 100 g (4 oz) polyester wadding might be used.

To prepare panels for quilting, place each piece of backing, wadding and top fabric together and tack securely all around. Tack along the centre lines and then across to create quarters.

Quilt the cover or cushion panels before making up, but after the first fit. Measure and pin the lines to be stitched and mark with a fabric marking pencil or tack in a contrasting colour. Hand or machine stitch through all layers, always starting from the same edge. Avoid puckers by holding the fabrics firmly at either side, and stitching slowly. Hand stitching will be slower, but there will be no danger of puckering and you can use heavier threads, jute string, wools and even decorative stitches.

CUSHIONS

Boxed, Turkish and wrap-around cushions can be used together well if the styles of furniture are mixed compatibly.

Early sofas were made with just one cushion on the seat, constructed of horsehair stitched into a mattress ticking cover. Although undoubtedly gaining a more comfortable resting place than the wooden or tightly upholstered seat beneath, by today's squashy, feather/down/fibre combinations, this method of seating can only be considered extremely unwelcoming.

However, there are times when the style of a piece of furniture has to be more important than the comfort. In such cases, I have covered horsehair pads with either a down quilt or a wool pad, both of which become tolerably comfortable without spoiling the traditional lines.

The most comfortable and manageable fillings have a high proportion of down. A mix of 85 per cent down with 15 per cent curled feathers provides a beautifully soft filling which moulds easily around the body, returning to shape almost immediately you leave it. However, down is rare and expensive and the fillings can become more costly than the sofa.

Try to aim for a 60 per cent down and 40 per cent feather combination – or a less expensive but heavier 40 per cent 60 per cent down/feather. The generally offered 85 per cent feather and 15 per cent down is not really acceptable, as the cushions become flat very quickly and are then difficult to handle and heavy to lift as you try to pummel new life back in. If this sounds familiar and your cushions are fairly new, try removing about 30 per cent of the feathers and replace them with down. If your cushion pads are old and heavy, the curled feathers will have degenerated into a flat, unresponsive form, incapable of holding any air, and the whole pad should be changed.

BOXED CUSHIONS

Boxed cushions are formal and traditional but allow ample opportunity for detailed finish. Use contrast fabrics for gussets or piping, stitch ruched braid, cords or flat braid instead of piping. Fit decorative buttons, ties, rouleaux or toggles for decorative closures. Quilting in any form, appliqué and many other hand-worked finishes may be applied or stitched for an individual touch.

MAKING UP

1. Cut out the pieces and make up piping following the instructions on page 8.

2. Place the top and bottom pieces flat on to the worktable, exactly together. Snip irregular marks on all four sides using single, double and triple cuts at 10–20 cm (4–8 in) intervals.

3. Starting on the back edge, pin piping to the right of the fabric, all round the top and bottom pieces. Pin so that the stitching line will be on the seam allowance. At the corners, snip right up to stitching line on the piping, open out the cut so that the piping forms a tight corner. Pin securely. Join the piping as instructed on page 8.

Jacket tweeds make wonderful hard-wearing cushions. Here, trimmed with leather, the overall effect with the silk paisley shawl and a touch of leopard skin is extremely smart.

4. Stitch on the piping. Insert the zip into the gusset strip following the instructions that are given on page 9. Join to the other gusset piece.

5. Starting with the free end of the gusset, pin one side of the gusset to the top of the cover. Match the seam allowance and then pin on to the piping line. Cut into the corners, right up to the seam allowance, to give a good square corner.

6. Where the zip gusset and the main gusset meet, pin together and stitch the short seam before finishing the pinning. Cut away any excess fabric. Stitch all round as close to the piping as possible. Check from the front that the first piping stitching line is not actually visible. If it is, stitch around again from the other side, making sure that your stitching line is inside the first one.

7. Pin the other side of the cover to the opposite side of the gusset. Start at the back and, matching the seam allowances, pin along the piping line. Match up the notched marks by scoring a pin line from a notch on the stitched side, across the gusset, following the fabric grain. At each corner score a pin line from the stitched corner to the opposite side of the gusset to align the corners exactly. Snip into the seam allowance. This cut should form the corner. Stitch the cover all around.

8. Cut across the corners to within 5 mm (¼ in) of the stitching. Neaten the seam, open up the zip and turn the cover to the right side. Push each corner to a good shape with a point turner or the end of the scissors. Press all over. Lightly press the seam allowances away from the gusset. Fill the cover with the pad, checking that the filling fits right into each corner.

TURKISH CUSHIONS

Turkish cushion covers, with their particular pleated or lightly gathered corners, fit over the same boxed pads but lend an informal air, most suited to a country fabric or cover. The fronts and backs are cut to fit over the pad and meet along the centre line of the gusset. The easiest way to make sure the corners are perfect is to fit the cover over the cushion pad. Once the four sides are pinned, take up the corner excess with a single pleat, an inverted pleat or a series of small gathers depending how casual the finish is to be. Self-pipe, or hand stitch cord over the seam. Finish with a knot at each corner.

WRAP-AROUND COVERS

Informal and easy-to-make cushion covers, suitable for the complete amateur and those frightened of piping, wrap-around covers depend only on side gussets and a simple closure.

Cut one length of fabric from the centre back gusset along the cushion length, under and around to meet at the centre back. Allow 2 cm (¾ in) at each end for closure allowance. Cut the fabric to the cushion width plus 2 cm (¾ in) seam allowance on each side. Pin over the pad and adjust the back closure seam for a good fit. Remember that the pad is always approximately 10 per cent larger than the finished cover, so fit the cushion into the chair seat to check the fit.

Cut a gusset for each side, the depth and length of the cushion side plus seam allowances. Pin the gussets along each side, keeping the back ends square but easing the fronts to make curved ends. Adjust until a good fit is obtained, trim seam allowances to 2 cm (¾ in), and mark at regular points with coloured tacks. These will help you to realign the pieces once the pins have been removed.

Insert a zip or make a placket for hooks and bars or ties along the closure seam. Open up and pin the side gussets in place, making sure the easement at each gusset front is neat, and any marking tacks are matched. Stitch together, neaten seams and then turn right side out.

If you would like to pipe the side gussets, do so before pinning them back to the main cover.

Wrap-around cushion covers with side gussets are informal and suit squashy country chairs and sofas. Useful also for window seats and Lloyd Loom style chair seats, they are often buttoned through.

FINISHING DETAILS

Dimity print wallpaper is the backdrop to this charming medley of patterns which combines an antique Northumbrian quilt, monochrome roses and a smart rock stripe.

Informal loose covers or slip-over covers offer many opportunities for additional detailed decoration. Free from the restrictions of tailored cutting when form is imposed by the line of the furniture beneath, the shaping and cutting of informal covers can be quietly restrained or elaborate in the extreme. A keen loose cover maker might like to experiment with more complicated shaping and draping, reflecting details from couture garments.

A wooden kitchen chair can be transformed with a loose cover; by barely following the original shape it can be given a character all its own. Armchair covers, too, can be made baggy and informal – especially useful if the shape below has deteriorated beyond that which a fitted cover could enhance.

Disproportionate or ugly chair legs can be conveniently disguised with a well-proportioned valance. My preference is always to make deep valances. I dislike the standard 15 cm (6 in) variety generally on offer – too short a valance can look 'stuck on' and out of balance. Whether straight or gathered, I much prefer the effect and balance when a skirt is taken from the seat or from just below the front roll.

Buttons in any shape, form, texture and size – toggles, frogging, ribbons and braids – can all be successfully employed to maximise the individuality and character of different chairs.

ARMCHAIR DETAILS

1. Gingham check from hotel suppliers is certainly inexpensive and hard-wearing, being manufactured specifically for intensive use and laundering.

Shaped to fit along the top roll and around the arms, the bottom and back were left loose for informality and ease of removal. This chair in my kitchen suffers daily abuse from children and pets, but after constant washing and pressing still looks good.

Flat piping and the back ties are interesting details.

2. Although cut to fit the chair, a nursery cover needs to be casual and simple to slip on and off for cleaning. For ease, the arms were made slightly loose and the skirt frilled from the seat. Nursery fabrics must be washable – I always think it is safer to pre-wash. Most fabrics will shrink a little in both directions, so don't just allowing extra on the length. Remember also only to use preshrunk piping cords and to launder linings before cutting.

3. Another chair in the same nursery asked for a different treatment. Inset gussets at each corner have piped sides which spring out to give body and shape to the skirt hem. The cover was pinned to fit the chair as a tailored cover, but each seam was eased 1 cm (⅜ in) before trimming.

4. Ticking is hard-wearing and available in interesting colours and varied stripes. Antique tickings from northern France, hand-woven cloths from Mediterranean islands and other ethnic weaves are often tough enough to make good covers. Some tightly woven fabrics can be hard to pin and stitch. Also check out the creasing factor – crush a square in your hands and see how quickly creases fall out. Always pre-launder an unknown fabric.

5. This idea was taken from an old, favourite jacket – two fabrics with the same weight and fibre content cover an antique French chair whose velvet upholstery I did not wish to remove. Fabric-covered buttons and hand-stitched buttonholes reflect further details.

6. Playing with contrasting fabrics and turning stripes are part of the fun of making loose covers. Centre seams are essential in this chair to take up the back curve.

1

2

3

4

5

6

WOOD
FRAMES

Underneath, a show wood Louis XV sofa is in good repair having been recently upholstered in a traditional stripe. Ochre-dyed toile de jouy also makes a perfect slip-over cover for alternative use.

Sofas, armchairs, garden chairs, kitchen and dining chairs with wood frames are more difficult to loose cover than chairs which are fully upholstered. But, with a little more preparation, results are very satisfying, and loose covers that just slip over make pleasant seasonal or occasion alternatives. Wood-framed chairs sporting casual fabric covers suggest a softer and more relaxed atmosphere.

Covers cannot be pinned tightly enough to make fitted covers, as there will be pulls and creases which cannot easily be pinned out – problems which can only be mastered by an extremely experienced maker. So choose heavily textured fabrics and all-over patterns so that the overall shape of the cover is more important than the details and finishes. You can just see the striped fabric beneath, but this doesn't matter at all given the change in formality which the loose cover has advanced.

All-white covers look tremendous in a summer holiday house, but lightly coloured fabrics and lightly printed patterns cannot be expected to hide fully the winter upholstery beneath. Only if the under-covers are really dark would I fit an unpiped calico cover over the upholstery first.

Tailoring details can be incorporated most effectively to chair backs and plain fabrics can be enriched from a structured treatment – if you have the experience and the will.

MAKING UP

Loose covers over wood chairs are made in exactly the same way as for upholstered chairs. Fabric pieces are planned in the same manner. Each piece needs to be pinned to the chair for the fitting and then together along each seam line.

To make this possible, fabric lengths or woven tapes are used to bind the frame. Whether cane, metal or wood, all frames are treated in the same way. On a free piece of wood, tapes can be tied around and knotted or pinned in place (see page 54). All tapes need to be tightly fixed, so that they do not swivel around as you pull on the fabric.

If the frame is old and tatty, you might be able to stick small pieces of woven tape to it, but if the upholstery meets the frame, tapes will need to be pinned to the upholstery on either side, stretched taut over the wood. You might be able to use tacks or drawing pins to hold the tape to the underside of the chair. But if all else fails, the chair will need to be bandaged from top to bottom and side to side.

For similar covers, make a seat template (see page 13) and cut two pieces of linen with a 1.5 cm (⅝ in) seam allowance all around. Make up two skirts, one to fit between the back legs and one for the rest of the seat.

Prepare piping (see page 8) and stitch to one of the seat pieces, 1.5 cm (⅝ in) from the raw edges. Gather the skirts to fit and stitch to the seat along the piping stitching line. Pin rouleau ties to either side of the back legs, and stitch securely with several rows of a zigzag or back stitch. Place the other seat piece over, right sides together, enclosing all seams. Stitch together, leaving a small opening at the back. Neaten seams, cut away corners and snip into curves. Turn out, press and slip stitch the opening.

Right: Organza is draped over the chair and knotted at the back to add a frothiness which can be fun for some occasions.

Below: Seat covers for a set of antique French dining chairs protect the upholstery beneath. Crisp white linen launders easily, returning fresh time and again. An organdie border is stitched to the line with a decorative stitch in perlé thread.

SINGLE CHAIRS

You can have fun with fabrics when covering single chairs. The chair on the right is covered with tailoring linen which is finely woven with a lovely glaze which crackles a little when creased. A fitted back and seat give way to a fully gathered skirt with the cascade of pintucks stitched to the lower half. At the back, a centre pleat punctuated with a hand-made ceramic button opens to show off the pintucked skirt.

On the left, an 'unfitted cover' used to wrap a Victorian lady's balloon-backed chair was cut from a single length of fabric. Pin to the inside and outside back, and push as much as possible into the seat 'tuck-in' to hold the fabric firmly in place. Pull the hanging flaps at each side to the back and pin together. Pencil curves around the seat front and on the floor at the back. Pin to check that the fabric hangs comfortably and then cut away. Bind all around with a similar or complementary fabric.

A bow made from the same fabric as the binding was stitched to hold the ends at the centre back.

LLOYD LOOM CHAIRS

Genuine Lloyd Loom chairs crop up in antique or junk shops all over the world. Originally made in Britain, these chairs are small and light enough to transport easily and be useful in many situations. Copies and similar style chairs are still being made fifty years later, as the Lloyd Loom style has found universal favour whether in the bathroom, kitchen, bedroom, sitting room, guest bedroom, and even the dining room.

In various states of disrepair, Lloyd Looms are normally rejuvenated with a coat of paint and a new seat – a loose cover presents a plausible option.

MAKING UP

1. Plan the pieces to cut following the principles detailed on pages 12–13. Allow double fullness for the skirt. Cane or 'basket' type chairs have no place for pins, so bind the whole chair as if bandaging; or if the frame is already in poor repair, stick narrow tape around the edge.

2. Cut one piece of fabric for the inner back and seat and pin to the outside edge all around. Pin away the excess until the fabric lies completely flat against the seat back and on to the seat.

3. Pin narrow binding tape around the raw edge to prevent the towelling from stretching.

4. Pin the skirt to the seat and back all around, taking up the fullness into pleats. These can be quite random, so don't spend too much time trying to make them all the same size. Trim back to allow a seam allowance of just under 2 cm (¾ in).

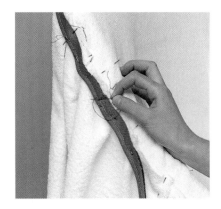

5. Make up enough piping to fit all round the seat and back. Pin to each pleat. Carefully unpin the pleated skirt and stitch the piping to hold the pleats in place. Stitch the seat seams, and then stitch the inner back and seat piece to the piping. Refit the cover to the chair and mark the hemline. Stitch with a double row of machine stitches 5 mm (¼ in) apart.

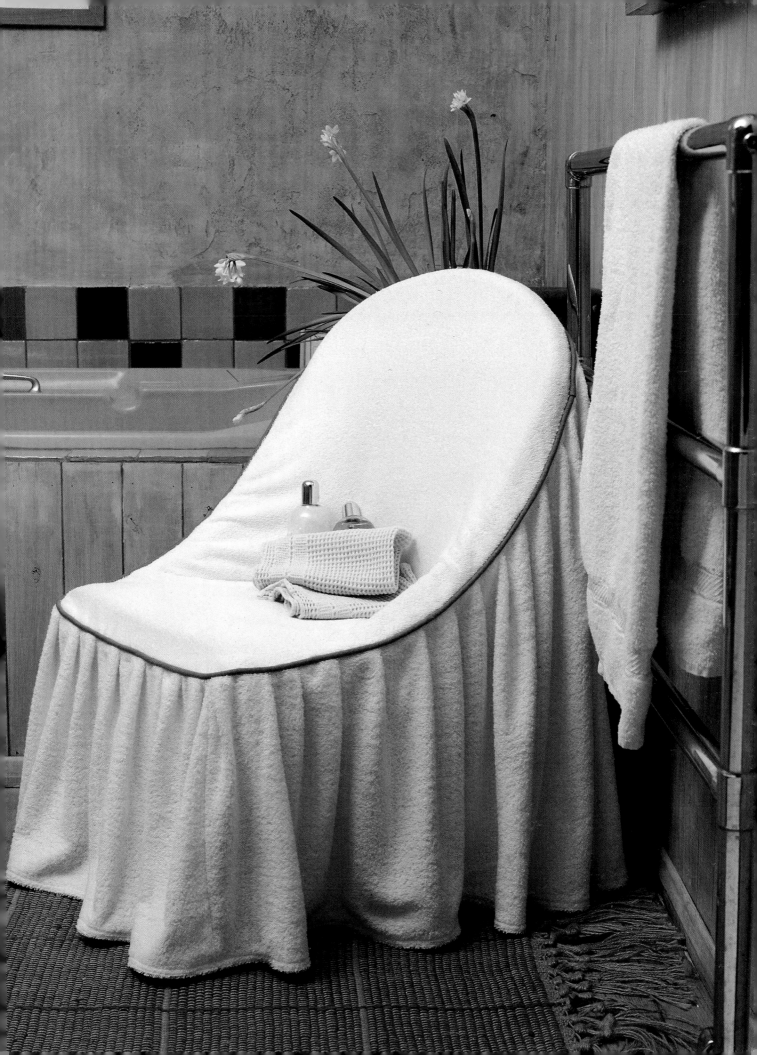

DAY BEDS

Strong ticking stripes from Normandy in a traditional brown and cream combine perfectly with toile de jouy printed with scenes from La dame du Lac in its original colouring. The day bed could be fully loose covered or, as here, part loose cover with skirts on either side of the seat.

Attractively designed day beds can quickly be turned into temporary or permanent seating with the addition of covers and cushions. Day beds can be entirely loose covered, perhaps in warm, sensuous fabrics: choose from damasks in wool, silk or cotton, tapestries, velvets, wools, tartans and plaids in plain and multi colours. Or select simple fresh stripes, checks, crisp linens or even filmy, ethereal fabrics such as organdie, muslin and linen scrims.

Very fine open weave linen scrim would look marvellous over these painted bed ends, tied at the sides, but loose enough for the colours and pattern to show through. Or full covers can completely transform a bed with plain or poor-quality head and foot boards.

To fit the covers the frame needs to be first bound with woven tape or lengths of fabric to provide an anchor for the pins (see page 54). Short valances enhance the shape and character of wooden day bed frames. If you want to use filmy fabrics then a gathered valance behind the side rails would be most appropriate.

A hint of the frame style should always remain – whether glimpsed through an open-weave cover or peeping through cut-out shapes.

KITCHEN AND DINING CHAIRS

I favour simple checks purchased from a hotel supplier for my farmhouse kitchen. Secure that these commercial fabrics have been manufactured specifically for hard wear and frequent laundering, I can leave them in place whatever the age and number of family and guests eating with us.

Every country in the world has its own indigenous style of kitchen chair, mostly made of wood but some wicker or cane. Whether French, Dutch, Scandinavian, English, North American, Greek, Italian, Spanish, each evokes a definite style in the mind's eye if used as a description of an ordinary wooden chair. Unfortunately, although lovely to look at, many of these are uncomfortable to sit on for any period of time, as the chair seats are usually constructed from wood or woven rushes.

As life becomes less formal, many of us now entertain so much more in the kitchen – morning coffee, a glass of wine after work or family suppers. Because of this, some sort of comfortable seat pad becomes essential. Squab cushions are flat pieces of foam or stitched hair, made to fit the seat shape, covered in fabric and tied to the legs at the back of the chair. They can be made as simply or as decoratively as you prefer, and may themselves have slip-over covers for use on different occasions.

Kitchen chairs may also be entirely or partially slip-covered. I now keep several sets of covers to cope with many occasions, from a children's party, to Christmas, summer supper or winter drinks. Once you have made an initial pattern and have practised on the first set, each further cover takes only a short while to make – a set can be easily completed within a day or in a couple of evenings.

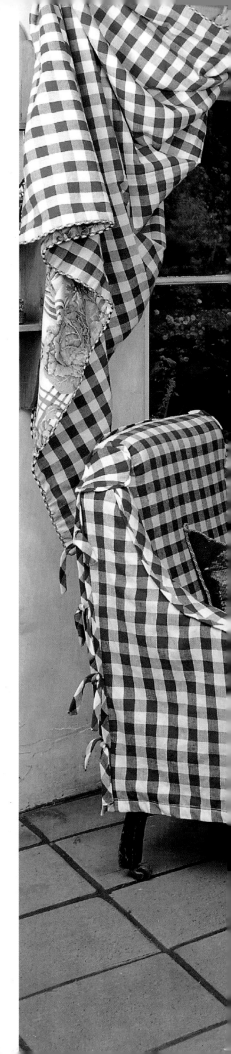

MAKING UP

Plan the amount of fabric needed following the same principles for all loose covers (see pages 12–13) and use calico to make the templates. You will find that wood-framed chairs need to be bound with lengths of fabric to provide an anchor for pinning.

1. Stitch tapes tightly in place to stop swivelling as pinned fabrics pull against each other. Drawing pins can hold tapes on old frames. Sticky tape can be used, but may remove paint.

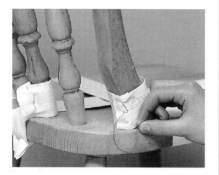

2. For a seat template, pin some calico to the taped edges. Push a pencil into the fabric around the back legs and cut calico to shape. Pencil around chair seat's edge and cut fabric along line. Check that the template is fixed and follows the seat shape. Put a note on the calico to add seam allowances.

3. Cutting the back is a little more difficult if you have not made enough pinning points. (This cover should fall loosely, but the template cover must fit quite tightly.) The front and back pieces at the top of the chair must be pinned together close to the frame and the fabric at each side must be equal. Trim seams to 2 cm (¾ in) and make notches and marking tacks to assist you when stitching pieces together – always mark any easement. Cut around the seat without seam allowances, but cut a 2 cm (¾ in) seam allowance for the back and front piece – note it in pencil on the template.

4. Cut out fabric pieces for the inner back, outer back, seat skirt and two plackets. Add seam allowances where necessary. This skirt was cut 20 cm (8 in) long to allow 4 cm (1½ in) for the hem and 2 cm (¾ in) for the seam allowance. Make up flat piping. Cut fabric strips on the cross 5 cm (2 in) wide and press in half.

5. Stitch the inner back to the seat and neaten the seam. Pin flat piping to the outer back all around, making small tucks at the top corners and stitch in place. Pin the inner back to the stitching line and ease or pleat the fullness around the top. Stitch flat piping around the seat and along the hemline of the outer back. To make up the skirts, make 2 cm (¾ in) double hems to finish. Stitch gathering threads along the top, pull up and pin to the seat and back, distributing the gathers evenly.

6. Make ties (see page 8) – four or six for each side. Pin one 3 cm (1¼ in) below the top opening, one at the top of the skirt and one in between if needed. Make a placket (see page 9) and pin over the ties. As you stitch the placket in place, triple stitch backwards and forwards over the ties to hold them securely in place.

The seam joining the seat to the inner back should fit snugly to the wood. Flat piping, cut on the cross, between the seat and the skirt makes an attractive finish.

A placket stitched around the back opening encloses all raw edges and secures the fabric ties.

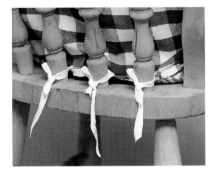

Long tapes need to be stitched to the inner back/seat seam and tied to each chair back strut to prevent the seat moving. You can just see the ticking squab which sits on the seat, under the loose cover.

This simple cover reminds me of a horse blanket – reversible, easy to store when not in use and very simple to make. Place the seat template on to the fabric and cut around the back with no allowance for seams. Add 12 cm (5 in) to the sides and front, following the curves and shape of the template. Stitch petersham ribbon or bias binding all around and make ties for the back legs to secure the cover to the seat.

CREATING A DINING SET

Once you have cut the first pattern and completed your first covers, you might be inspired to make more sets for other occasions.

Instead of making up a separate frilled skirt, add 18 cm (7 in) to the outer back length and around the three sides of the seat template. A stencilled design can be painted on to each piece before stitching together. Use fabric paints, dry and press under a clean cloth with a hot iron. A simple hem was stitched all around and the back openings stitched together. Fabric-covered buttons stencilled with a miniature grape design hold small pleats at both legs.

For a tailored fit (above), the back was cut into three panels, shaped to take up the fullness. The two pleats were created by leaving the back seams open beyond the seat. Pretty stencilled fabric buttons define the pleats and punctuate the plain cream.

To make a back opening (right), the outer back template is cut through the centre and 8 cm (3¼ in) added to both sides. Instead of the frilled skirt, add 18 cm (7 in) to the length. Also add 18 cm (7 in) to three sides of the seat template. Make up the outer back first. Press extra fabric under, 2 cm (¾ in) from centre back line. Neaten raw edges. Pin together two layers, lining up centres and overlapping by 4 cm (1½ in). Make buttonholes on top piece and stitch covered button-holes on under piece.

Make up the cover as before, stitching the backs to the hem.

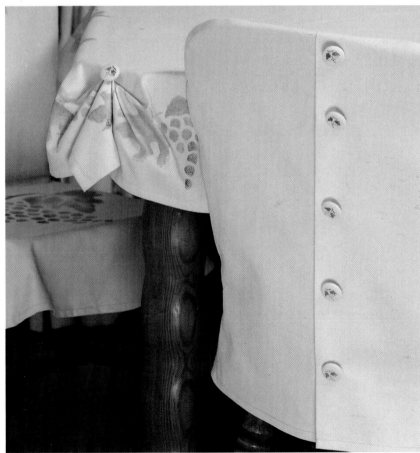

FORMAL DINING CHAIRS

Dining chairs usually have comfortable upholstered seats, and antique chairs especially are ideal for a premium fabric. These type of chairs need only a little fabric which generally is seen rather than used. However, unavoidable spills will demand that a practical fabric should be considered.

Putting loose covers on dining chairs is a good solution as slip-over covers can be permanent or temporary features. They can be removed to launder, or put on and off for dinner parties and Sunday lunch. Costly upholstery fabrics are then saved from damage and should last as long as the original upholstery underneath.

The most comfortable dining chairs to accommodate our rather informal way of life and extended seating at table are not antique, but new and fully upholstered. These can be ordered upholstered in your own fabric or in calico with removable slip covers. In any case, more than one set of covers can transform your dining room for any situation. Richly coloured Highland plaid fitted covers are excellent for the colder seasons, while blue and white stripes loosely fitted and held together with ties are excellent spring and summer furnishings.

A Highland plaid in rich blues and reds, threaded with olive green, covers soft caramel upholstery for the Christmas period. The addition of red ties and piping is warm and seasonal.

DESIGN AND MAKE LOOSE COVERS

1

2

GARDEN GALLERY

1. Quilted, padded covers in bright, café cloth, instantly dress these chairs in picnic mood. Cut two pieces of fabric long enough to cover the outside and inside backs and the seat length, with enough overlap to pad the back of the knees. Measure the chair's widest part and use this for the width. Add 5 per cent for quilting 'shrinkage' and 1.5 cm (⅝ in) all around for seam allowance. Make a long strip of binding to fit all around, cut on the cross. Press this binding in half and stitch to the front of the top cover piece, 1.5 cm (⅝ in) from the raw edges. Place the back piece over with right sides together and stitch

around three sides, leaving one short edge to pull the cover to the right side. Stitch a length of 150 g (6 oz) polyester wadding to the whole piece using the same seam allowance. Trim seams, turn and press, slipstitch the opening. Plan three squares for quilting the seat and backs. Stitch through all layers so that the covers are completely reversible. Slip on to the chair and mark the tie positions. Insert eyelets and thread self fabric or tape ties through.

2. To add a little more comfort for a lingering summer lunch, I wanted a cover that would be attractive and disguise any scatter cushion that had been slipped on to the chair seat.

The inner and outer backs are

cut in one length, and stitched from the top to the seat on both sides. Cut the seat piece to fit over a plump pad, making tucks at each front corner and cutting around the back legs. Leave approximately 8 cm (3 in) to slip down behind the cushion at the back of the chair. Ties will be stitched to this flap to hold the cover to the chair seat, preventing the cushion walking forwards.

Pipe around the seat and along the bottom of the back piece. Make two skirt pieces with double hems stitched and gathered up to about twice fullness to fit along the back and around the seat. Stitch to the piping just inside the last stitching line. Neaten all seams and raw edges and stitch ties to

3

4

the inside back to hold to the chair. Stitch self fabric to the two back seams for decoration and tie into generous bows or loops.

3. These simple seat and back covers can be adapted to fit most chairs. Contrast plain fabrics with checks, florals and stripes.

Make a template of the seat size and cut a piece of 1 cm (⅜ in) thick foam to this pattern. For each seat, cut two fabric pieces, adding 1 cm (⅜ in) all around to allow the foam pad to slide in and 8–15 cm (3–6 in) along the sides and front, for the 'skirt'. Cut any shaping and allow 1.5 cm (⅝ in) for each seam. With right sides together, stitch around three sides and the length of the 'skirts' on the back edge. Turn out, press,

place the foam pad over and mark the position. Stitch around three sides to keep the pad in place, insert the pad and slipstitch the back closed. Mark the position for the ties and make eyelets to hold the seat cover to the chair back.

4. This is a simple chair cover to make as only two seams are needed or none if you use extra wide fabric. Think of each section as a square, the outer back, inner back, seat, front skirt and two side skirts. The back, the seat and the front skirt are cut in one piece, with the two side skirts joined to the seat. Take one measurement from the floor at the back up to the top of the chair, down to the seat, across the seat and down to the floor at the front. Cut some

fabric the width of the chair plus 8 cm (3¼ in) and the measured length plus 8 cm (3¼ in). Mark the top of the chair, back and front and back of the seat section with pins or marking tacks. Cut two side skirts, with 8 cm (3¼ in) extra width and 6 cm (2¼ in) extra length. If the chair seat slopes backwards, trim the top to fit as these pieces will not be quite square. Stitch the top of each side skirt between the marked back and front seat section, placing the skirts so that the seams are 3 cm (1¼ in) in from each side. Make double hems all around using the 6 cm (2¼ in) allowed on the sides and the 4 cm (1½ in) for the hems. Attach ties to hold the cover at the back and front legs.

MAKING UP

1. These covers fit over two inexpensive director's chairs. Cut a template in calico or an old sheet first to help you plan the centre seam and arm facings. Cut the outer back the width of the chair plus 4 cm (1½ in) for seam allowances on each side and hem and 2 cm (¾ in) at the top. Cut one piece long enough to cover the inner back, seat and to the floor, the width of the chair plus 8 cm (3 in) at each side, 2 cm (¾ in) at the top and 4 cm (1½ in) at the hem.

2. Cut two pieces for the inner arms, adding 20 cm (8 in) to the front edge and two pieces for the outer arms, the width of the arms plus 4 cm (1½ in) at each side.

From each of the main fabrics, cut one side of the inner back and seat, one side of the outer back, one inner arm and one outer arm. Also make four ties, following the colour scheme here if you wish.

3. Join the centre seams of the inner and outer backs. Press flat and top stitch. Join the inner and outer arm pieces and finish in the same manner.

4. Pin the inner and outer backs together at the top of the chair, from above each arm, making a pleat on the front piece at the top corner. Remove and seam.

5. Place the arm pieces over, with the 'flaps' of the inner arm at the front. Pin the inner arm to the seat and inner back. Remove cover and make seams. Make 2 cm (¾ in) double hems all around the raw edges. Fit cover back on and pin the positions of the ties. Double stitch these in place.

6. Inside the cover, stitch lengths of tape to the seat seams which will tie around the chair arms and legs to prevent the cover slipping.

Full covers completely disguise rather uninteresting plastic chairs. Skirts cut to finish 2.5–5 cm (1–2 in) off the floor avoid the early morning dew. Pink and white stripes look stunning in midsummer and in evening light for garden suppers.

STOOLS

The simplest cover is a square or rectangle tied to fit snugly over the stool beneath. Hems may be finished with braids or other decoration, corners rounded and rouleau ties, cords or, as here, plaited suede used to hold the cover in place decoratively.

Stools are such useful small accessories in any living room, providing valuable additional seating for a small guest or family member at busy times. If firmly upholstered, a stool can be pressed into service as a spare table and perhaps as a centre coffee table when necessary. As a foot rest placed in front of an armchair, a stool can extend the use to a day bed, providing welcome rest at the close of a busy day or to a house-bound patient. Tucked into a corner, placed in front of bookshelves, beside a fireplace or in a cupboard when not in use, stools are no trouble to accommodate, being easy to manoeuvre to the point of need.

As with all loose covers, stool covers may be tailored and fitted or loose, buttoned or tied and held at each corner. Tailored covers follow the shape of the stool, usually with a skirt and often with a gusset at the top which helps to keep the cover in place.

Loose covers are chosen for practicality or camouflage. Choose your fabrics carefully to perform the necessary function well. Washable fabrics need to be selected for hard-wear areas such as nurseries; heavy textured fabrics are best to disguise a battered item. Stools can successfully be made from old boxes with a little padding fixed to the lid.

The simplest stool covers are squares or rectangles thrown over and tied at each corner. Piped, bound, lined, unlined, buttoned, tied or laced, the fabric mix and detail of finish are limited only by time and imagination.

FITTED STOOL COVERS

Fitted stool covers benefit from the inclusion of a gusset of some depth to hold the cover firmly over the top 'cushion'. A skirt can then be attached to reach the floor or, if the legs are good, just long enough to cover the upholstery.

If the stool design suggests just a top and skirt, stitch tapes into each corner long enough to tie underneath, so preventing the cover sliding around.

MAKING UP

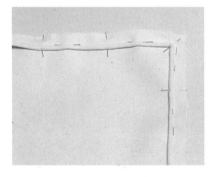

1. Measure, plan and cut the top, gusset and skirt pieces following the principles on pages 12-13. Make up the skirt (see page 21), marking each corner clearly.

Make up enough piping to fit twice around the stool. Place the top piece on to the worktable and pin the piping around. Keep the corners square and join neatly following the instructions on page 21.

Always plan and design any cover to suit your fabric. These boxed pleats have been placed to do full justice to both small and large teddies.

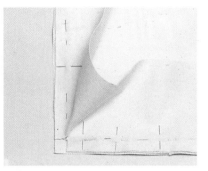

2. Stitch in place. Pin the gusset to the piping line, snipping into the corners sharply, keeping the fabric flat to either side. Join the gusset seam. Stitch along the piping stitching line. Check from the right side to make sure that the first stitching line does not show and if it does, stitch around again closer to the piping.

3. Stitch the remaining piping to the bottom of the gusset. Pin the valance around and tack securely.

4. Fit the cover on to the stool to make sure the length is correct. Stitch close to the piping and again if any stitches still show from the front of the cover.

UNFITTED STOOL COVERS

Squares or rectangles tied, buttoned or knotted over the stool are effective, inexpensive, straight-forward to make and practical to launder. Use fabrics that work with your other soft furnishings: scarves, small sofa throws or blankets, lap rugs or even antique floor rugs are all highly suitable and can be pressed into use.

1. The simplest stool cover ever made – measure from just below the upholstery, over the top to the same distance below the upholstery on the other side. Cut one square or rectangle to these measurements plus seam allowances for the top cover and one for the lining. Using fabric of an equal quality (here to match the sofa cover) gives opportunity to ring the changes.

Place the two fabrics together, right sides facing, and stitch all around, leaving a 15 cm (6 in) opening. Trim corners, pull right side out, press and slip stitch to close the gap. Fit over the stool and stitch buttons to hold the corner pleats. Just remove the buttons for laundering.

2. Linen printed with roses is lined in a smart cotton stripe, which also binds the hemline. As it is cut on the cross it adds an extra dimension. Rouleau ties hold each corner and pleats are encouraged to fall informally. As an interesting alternative, fabric-covered buttons and tiny rouleau loops hold the chair skirt firmly behind.

3. This cover has been made reversible with a plain linen lining and a continuing decorative binding equally on the other side. Also cut as a square or rectangle, the corners were then cut away to take in the stool legs. The top and under fabrics were placed together with wrong sides inward, bound with fabric cut on the cross 6 cm (2¼ in) wide (see page 9). To hold cover in place, rouleau ties were laced through brass eyelets and criss-crossed down each leg.

DRAPED COVERS

A rose stitched from pink silk nestles in apricot bows, twisted easily from organdie ribbon - blissful for a summer christening party.

A single length of cotton organdie was draped over the back of the chair (right) and pinned so that the front just covered the seat and frame. At the back 30 cm (12 in) extra was allowed for the pintucks. The two spare corners at the front were pulled to the back of the chair and tied together. The folds and gathers that appear need to be pinned in place to look as natural as possible. Although these pleats should look uncontrived, if there were not some restraint they would fall out each time the chair was moved.

The curved hem from centre back to seat front might need to be cut to shape – just trim away the two corners.

Remove the organdie 'cover'. Stitch the pintucks and make hems all around. Replace the organdie and secure the back pleats with safety pins or small stitches. Tie the corners over these fixings and add decoration to suit the occasion.

Any soft fabric could be substituted – deep red silk for Christmas, pale pink for a Christening, a silver or gold print to celebrate a wedding anniversary.

MAKING UP

1. Take measurements and plan cuts as pages 12–13. For this cover, the inner and outer back pieces are cut as one, with 50 cm (20 in) extra allowed at each side. The inner and outer arm pieces are also cut as one, with 40 cm (16 in) extra allowed at the front arm and 20 cm (8 in) at the back. The seat piece is extended at the front and sides to fall to the floor.

2. Make up Turkish or wrap-around cushion covers. Make up four bows each about 20 x 8 cm (8 x 3 in).

3. Join seams as necessary and pin the back and seat pieces to the sofa. Pin together along the back tuck-in. Cut away at the arm front so that the side falls straight. Pin the hem in place along the floor. Trim the fabric along the seat/arm join so that 12 cm (4¾ in) only remains – this for the side tuck-in.

4. Pin the arm piece in place along the top of the sofa arm, and smooth down the inner arm to the seat tuck-in. Pin together along the tuck-in.

5. At the back of the outside arm, pin the 'flap' to the back of the sofa. Pin the back and arm pieces together to shape around the arm. This area needs to be cut well enough so that the arm and back fabrics lie comfortably, but the particular fitting needed for a tight cover is not necessary.

6. Stitch the tuck-ins and arm/back seam together. Neaten seams. Fit the cover back on to the sofa. Shape the excess fabric at the front arm so that the hemline drapes into a gentle curve to the floor. Gather the back pieces together and cut the hemline to drape softly. Remove the cover again and hem these and all other raw edges. Press thoroughly and fit the cover back on to the sofa.

7. Gather the fullness of each drape and stitch with double thread to hold. The flap which is at the back of each side should be pinned to the sofa back with upholstery pins, allowing the folds to hang over the back opening. Stitch rouleau bows over the gathering stitching.

Silk - spun and woven in the manner of linen - is convincing with its crunchy texture and matt finish, and is given away only by the extravagantly soft drapes. Fresh green revives the deep tan under-cover for spring and summer use.

DRESSING UP

Wonderfully informal covers can be made from simple throw sheets or antique bed linen. Or for unusual shapes, make up a straightforward cover, customized to shape.

To make a draped cover as shown at the top, measure the sofa, plan and cut the fabric pieces as pages 12–13. Include an extra 20–40 cm (8–16 in) at each end. Pin to the sofa, and join the seams of inside and outside backs, arms and tuck-ins around the seat. Fit the cover back on to the sofa, pin up the hems and stitch. Gather up the excess at each corner, hand stitch and finish with bows, ties, buttons or rose details.

Antique linen sheets make perfect squares for tied chair covers. Worn areas can be cut away, patched, hidden into folds or at worst, covered by a strategically placed cushion. In the picture immediately right a new, hand-embroidered sheet has been used with the beautiful stitchery taking pride of place. Just drape the sheet over the chair, level the front and side hems and push the excess fabric into the seat sides and back. If the cover drapes on to the floor at the back, trim away and hem. Alternatively, fold under and tack if you want to preserve the original size.

DESIGN AND MAKE LOOSE COVERS

CLEANING

To wash your loose cover, follow the manufacturer's instructions for the fabric and half dry as recommended. Press carefully. Press into the seams from either side with the point of the iron. Do not press over the seams as they will mostly have at least four layers of fabric and will mark the main cover with a ridge.

Sleeve back on to the chair while still damp. Finger press all seams in the same direction (usually to the back and down, although sometimes the shape of the chair demands otherwise). Pull cover into shape over curves and corners whilst still damp.

Press the cover while on the chair if needed. To press the valance after the cover has been fitted, plug your iron into a socket positioned close to the chair. Make a plain cotton pad and place on to a low stool, lift up the valance piece by piece and press.

GLOSSARY

FIBRES

Acrylic Manmade from petrol, often mixed with more expensive fibres to keep the cost down. Not particularly hardwearing.

Cotton A natural fibre, cotton is very versatile, woven, knitted and mixed with other fibres. It will lose strength in direct sunlight, so protect. Soft, strong, easy to launder, washable if pre-shrunk.

Linen Fibres found inside the stalks of the flax plant are woven to make linen cloth in almost any weight. Distinctive slub weave from very fine linen to a heavy upholstery weight. A very strong fibre which is easy to work and will take high temperatures.

Silk From the cocoon of the silk worm, silk is soft and luxurious to touch. Fades in sunlight, so protect. Available in every weight.

Wool A natural fibre, liable to excessive shrinkage as the 'scales' on each fibre overlap, harden and 'felt'. Is warm to touch and initially resists damp.

Viscose Wood pulp woven into fibres which mixes well with other fibres helping them to take dyes and fireproofing. Washable and sheds dirt easily.

FABRICS

Brocade Traditionally woven fabric using silk, cotton, wool or mixed fibres, on a jacquard loom, in a multi or self coloured floral design. Some are washable but most will need dry cleaning.

Calico Coarse, plain weave cotton in cream or white with 'natural' flecks in it. Available in many widths and weights. Wash before use to shrink and press damp.

Cambric Closely woven, plain weave fabric from linen or cotton with a sheen on one side. Use, wash and press as Calico.

Canvas Plain weave cotton in various weights. Available as unbleached, coarse cotton or more finely woven and dyed in strong colours.

Chintz Cotton fabric with Eastern design using flowers and birds, often with a resin finish which gives a characteristic sheen or glaze and which also repels dirt. The glaze will eventually wash out, so only dry clean. Avoid using steam to press and never fold or the glaze will crack.

Corduroy A strong fabric woven to form vertical ribs by floating extra yarn across which is then cut to make the pile. Press on a velvet pinboard while damp.

Crewel Plain or hopsack woven, natural cotton background embroidered in chain stitch in plain cream, wool or multi-coloured wools. Soft but heavy; may be washed, but test a small piece first.

Damask A jacquard fabric first woven in Damascus with satin floats on a warp satin background in cotton, silk, wool and mixed fibres in various weights. Make up reversed if a matt finish is required.

Gingham Plain weave fabric with equal width stripes of white plus one other colour in both warp and weft threads to produce blocks of checks or stripes in 100 per cent cotton. Mix with floral patterns and other checks and stripes.

Holland Firm, hardwearing fabric made from cotton or linen stiffened with oil or shellac.

Organdie The very finest cotton fabric with an acid finish giving it a unique crispness. Wash and press while damp.

Organza Similar to organdie and made of silk, polyester or viscose. Use layers of varying tones or pastel colours over each other.

Provençal prints Small print designs printed by hand on to fine cotton. Washable, hardwearing, soft and easy to work with.

Tartan Authentic tartans belong to individual Scottish clans and are woven or worsted fine twill weave with an elaborate checked design. Traditional wool tartans are hard-wearing.

Ticking Characteristic original herringbone weave in black and white, now woven in many colours and weights. Not usually pre-shrunk.

Toile de jouy Pastoral designs in one colour printed on to calico using copper plate printing.

Tweed Wool or worsted cloth in square or rectangular checked designs in few colours.

Velvet Originally 100 per cent silk, now made from cotton, viscose or other manmade fibres. Woven with a warp pile and additional yarn in loops to form a pile. Care needs to be taken when sewing or the fabrics will 'walk'. Press on a velvet pinboard. Dry clean carefully. Always buy good quality velvet with a dense pile which will not pull out easily.

A
Arm caps 27, 28
Armchairs 24, 25, 26, 31, 38, 39
   club 24
   covering 14-19
   details on 40-41
   estimating fabric for 12
Arm covers 27, 28
   cutting 27
Arm shapes 24-31
   club 25, 28
   finishing details for 26
   laid back 25, 28
   scroll 25, 28
   straight 25, 28

B
Balloon-back chair 47
Binding techniques 9, 21
Blanket stitch 6
Bows 28, 29, 46
Boxed cushions 36
Box pleats 23
Buttonhole stitch 6
Buttons 38

C
Calico 11, 12
Carver chair 61
Chairs 13, 14
   balloon-back 47
   carver 61
   desk 62
   dining 13, 56-63
   director's 68
   dressing table 4
   garden 64-69
   kitchen 13, 28, 38, 52-55
   Lloyd Loom 37, 48-49
      measuring and planning for 11, 12, 13
   nursery 40
   plastic 68
   winged 30, 31
   wooden 13, 38, 52-56
   wood-framed 42-49, 62-63
   see also armchairs
Chair seat, making template for 13
Cleaning loose covers 79
Club arm 25, 28
Club armchair 24
Colour schemes 4, 22
Corner-pleated valance 21, 22
Cotton fabric 5
Cushion fillings 34
Cushions 12
   boxed 34
   making 12, 34-37
   patterns for 11, 13
   squab 13, 52, 55

Turkish 34, 37
   wrap-around 34
Cutting out 12
   planning for 11, 12, 13

D
Day beds 50-51
Desk chair 62
Dining chairs 13, 56-63
Director's chair 68
Draped covers 4, 74-78
Dressing table chair 4

E
Equipment 10

F
Fabrics
   checking 10
   choosing 5
   cutting out 11, 12
Fillings for cushions 34
Finishing details 38-41
Flat fell seam 7
Flat seam 7
Folded ties 8
French seam 7
Frilled valance 21, 23

G
Garden chairs 64-69
Gingham check 40
Graph paper 12
Gussets 6

H
Hemming 6
Hemming stitch 6
Herringbone stitch 6
Hook and bar closure 9

K
Kitchen chairs 13, 28, 38, 52-55
Knife-pleated valance 23

L
Ladder stitch
Laid back arm 25, 28
Let-in flap 28, 29
Lined covers, sewing 6
Linen 5
Linen piqué 64
Linen union 5
Lloyd Loom chairs 37, 48-49

M
Martindale test 5
Measuring 12, 13
Mitred corners 7

N
Nursery chair 40

O
Organdie 44, 74
Organza 44, 45

P
Pattern matching 10
Patterns 10, 11, 12
Pinning 7
Plackets 6, 9, 55
Planning 12
Plastic chairs 68
Piping 11, 25, 26
   making 8

Q
Quilting 32, 33, 66

R
Raw edges, finishing 6
Rouleau ties 8, 28, 29
Rub test 5

S
Scroll arm 25, 28
Seams
   flat 7
   flat fell 7
   French 7
   self-piped 28, 29
Silk 4, 76
Skirts, see Valances
Slip stitch 6
Sofas 14, 27, 34
   covering 16-19
   planning covers for 11
Squab cushions 13, 52, 55
Stencil designs 57
Stitches
   blanket 6
   buttonhole 6
   hemming 6
   herringbone 6
   ladder 6
   slip 6
Stools 70-73
   fitted covers for 72
   unfitted covers for 73
Straight arm 25, 28

T
Tailored covers 14-19
   cutting out 16-17
   making up 18-19
Tailoring details 42
Tailoring linen 46
Ticking 40, 41
Ties
   folded 8
   making 8

rouleau 8, 28, 29
Toile 12
Towelling 48
Turkish cushions 37

U
Unlined covers, sewing 6, 7
Upholstered furniture, covering 14-41, 61, 62

V
Velvet 5
Valances 20-23, 38
   binding hem 21, 22
   corner-pleated 21
   frilled 21, 23
   knife-pleated 23
   stitches for 6, 7

W
Winged chairs 30, 31
Wooden chairs 13, 38, 52-56
Wood-framed chairs 42-49, 62-63
Worktable 10
Wrap-around cushion covers 34

Z
Zip, inserting 9